Stolen
The story of th

www.findspirit.co.uk

Copyright © Lisa Wasilewski 2016

All rights reserved. This book or any portion thereof may not be reproduced or used in any manner whatsoever without the express written permission of the publisher except for the use of brief quotation in a book review.

Some of the names and places have been changed to protect the identity of some of the people involved.

www.flyingspiritcreations.com

Spirit - My soul mate

Contents

Chapter One - The Obsession, Hopes and Dreams

Chapter Two - The Soul and Spirit Unite

Chapter Three - Stress Testing the Relationship

Chapter Four - From Better to Worse

Chapter Five - Emptiness Leads Me to Merlin

Chapter Six - Milagros

Chapter Seven - Horseless and Hopeless

Final Word

Acknowledgements

The Obsession, Hopes and Dreams

All of my life I have loved horses. It had become an obsession. I'm told that even as a baby, before I could even talk I would get really excited at the 'horse' page in farm picture books, and when the page was turned over I would turn it back to gaze at the horse for a long time! As a young girl I had My Little Ponies, hundreds of horse models and ornaments. My bedroom walls were lined with pictures and posters pulled from horsey books and magazines. I even wanted to be a horse! I would draw them, paint them and model them out of plasticine or lego. I loved craft and all of my craft projects were horse related like painting horseshoes, decorating mugs with horses on making horse jigsaws. Obsessed? Yes! And the obsession was here to stay! And that it did. It grew, stronger and stronger with each passing day, month and year, and with that it flourished.

As soon as I was old enough my mum took me for riding lessons. Being a single mum with two children we could only afford to go every two weeks and I was never allowed my own pony due to the cost of keeping one. I don't even recall my first ride let alone my first trot or canter as I was so young. However, the first ride I do remember was just magical. It felt so right to be sitting on top of a pony. This wonderful being that was so strong and powerful, yet gentle and kind. I took to it like a natural. I just wanted to ride all day, every day. I would get so excited before my lesson and to find out which pony I was riding. The feeling of arriving at the riding school was like having butterflies in my stomach. I would go to reception where the list of pony names was waiting. Sometimes it would be a disappointment if I was allocated a lazy pony but most of the time I was jumping about with excitement knowing I was going to have a great ride.

My mum often reminds me of the time I got bitten by a little black Shetland pony when I was about three and that it nearly took my hand off! We were visiting a garden centre where a few animals were in the pens near the entrance. I wanted to be like the other children who were feeding the pony with grass, and I followed mum's instructions when she explained that he would take it off my hand if I kept it absolutely flat. Well, I did follow mum's instructions but unfortunately the pony wasn't listening to her because he took my whole hand into his mouth and wouldn't let go! Mum was frantic, having visions of my fingers being completely bitten off. She repeatedly nudged his muzzle and tried to manually open his mouth while I became more distressed. In the end she had to drag my hand out simply to avoid me becoming permanently fingerless on one hand. The result was a badly grazed hand, quite a few tears and a mum who nearly had a heart attack!. I think it scared my mum more than it scared me though. She really thought that the experience would put me off horses for life! However that was not to be! As I grew older, my back garden would be transformed into an arena with jumps made out of garden chairs and sticks and whatever else I could find and my friends and I would play ponies and jump the jumps, making all the 'mistakes' horses would do… running out, knocking a pole, whinnying with excitement! Just the crazy things that kids do! I remember my dad, who is no longer in my life, found a box of horse tack in an empty house he was doing up and he gave it all to me. I would sit and clean it and look at it for hours, and so at an early age I could put a bridle together with my eyes closed. If only I had my own horse to use it all on!

I have a particularly clear memory of one of the riding lessons I had when I was about ten. The pony I was riding, Dapple, spooked when the horse in front kicked out at him causing me to lose my stirrups. He then reared and one of the stirrups flung up and hit me in the eye. I managed to stay on and I could feel my eye instantly swelling but I chose to stay on and carry on with the lesson. With only getting a lesson every two weeks I wasn't definitely not going to let something like that cut it short. I ended up with the biggest black eye I had ever known and all of my friends were really freaked out by it. They didn't want to sit next to me in school because it was so horrible. But to me it was just proof that horses would always be in my life and I would never be put off. There would be many accidents and injuries to come. As they say, many falls make you a better rider!

In my teenage years I would help at the local riding school on the weekends which I loved. It was hard work and the days were long but I didn't care as I just loved being around the horses and it meant I would get a riding lesson in return. I would do everything from mucking out, filling haynets, brushing and tacking up horses and leading in lessons. Even at this point when I realised just how much hard work goes into horses I wasn't put off. It drove me to keep following my dreams and do it more.

No one could ever have an idea of how ridiculously excited I became when my mum one day said that I could loan a pony for a few days a week. A friend of hers from work had a pony for her daughter who was busy with homework and exams and needed a helper to deal with him. I got to look after him and although he was also a bit small for me I loved him. It was an amazing opportunity. His name was Dandy, a little 13.2hh chestnut gelding who was so sweet. He was cheeky and a real character but safe and I trusted him. This was just amazing for me as I could stand and brush him all day and mess about with him. My childhood dreams were coming true. We went for long hacks on our own around the countryside back in the day when it was safe to do so. I learnt so much from Dandy, mainly how to ride bareback and not fall off! Sadly it was to be short lived though as the owners decided to sell him so I had to give him up. This truly upset me as I was back to square one again with no pony, back to just having riding lessons.

All the time I constantly pestered my mum for my own horse not knowing just what was involved financially and of course time as I would have to rely on her to get me to and from the horse and fit it all in around school, homework and my mum's and brother's needs. At that age you have no real concept of what adult life involves and why a horse is a massive commitment.

I felt like I would never have a horse of my own. I would trawl through the horses for sale adverts in the horse magazines, circling the ones I wanted, adding up my pocket money and convincing myself it would be possible to have one. I was actually torturing myself doing this as I would get myself all excited, my imagination would run wild thinking of how amazing it would be to do anything I wanted with my own horse. To ride around the countryside, take trips to the beach, brush him for hours and hours and then it would all come crashing down when reality kicked in.

Once I left school I found a job at Manchester Airport and worked there for several years doing various different roles. I had learnt from many people that there was no money working in the world of horses so I figured that getting a reasonably paid job would get me the horse I had longed for throughout my childhood. I would have loved to go to college to do equine studies and it is something I seriously looked into but I just wanted to earn the money to buy my own horse. I wanted to be a groom but it just didn't pay all that well.

The money did start coming in but at that age I was needing to buy a car and I found a boyfriend. Unfortunately he didn't share my passion for horses. We had holidays together over the years and my priorities in life changed so horses were put on hold but they were still there in my mind, silently growing, always there like a horse-shaped hole in my heart. Still an obsession. I could not truly suppress it and I had to keep something equine in my life. It WAS my life. I would try and ride regularly at the riding school but I didn't feel that my riding or experience was progressing.

Anyway, I just couldn't stay away! I took the risk and got myself a full time job as a groom and trained to be a riding instructor at a riding school in Carrington, Manchester. I was in my element! While working there it helped me to realise the money, time and commitment needed to keep a horse and it certainly wasn't a suitable path to go down for people who don't like mud or rain! A continuous supply of the welly boot is a must!

The pay there was not enough for me to buy and keep a horse though. I was sure my time would come so kept trying to save what money I could spare. At least I was around the horses and could ride and groom them without the commitment and expense.

I was 27 years old when I finally met a stunning PRE Andalusian gelding by the name of Dixey and his owner Joanne who came to the riding school as a livery. 27 years is a long time to wait when horses have been in your blood from birth! I was back working at the airport at this point for the better wage. I saw this as a great opportunity to get involved with horses again after just taking the odd lesson and perhaps offer to look after this horse for a few days each week. After some discussion with Joanne we decided to set up a loan agreement that I share Dixey and care for him three days a week. I was thrilled!

A PRE, meaning Pura Raza Espanola which is a purebred Spanish horse, had been the horse of my dreams for many years. Their beauty, strength and intelligence had captured my heart. Dixey was a fine example of the breed. Loaning Dixey meant I found a good friend in Joanne and we had plenty of fun with him. It was my first real taste of having a horse even if it was just for three days a week. He was entirely my responsibility for those days. So since giving up Dandy I was back to having a horse again which was the most wonderful feeling. Back to living my dream.

I now had the freedom to do what I wanted and go riding out with friends without any restrictions of the riding school. I made new friends this way and I leant so much more about horses and even riding.

After only three months of loaning Dixey, disaster struck. He suffered a serious bout of colic, a massive impaction in his gut. It was an awful experience finding him collapsed in the field. He collapsed three further times on the way in from the field where we waited for the vet. It was incredibly frightening at the time. It was my first experience of impaction colic and I wasn't sure how to deal with it as I couldn't get in touch with Joanne. This made me panic as the responsibility fell completely on my shoulders. I called the vet hoping they would come out for me without Joanne's authorisation. Fortunately they were happy to come out.

The vet took about half an hour to arrive during which I walked Dixey around in the arena to try and stop him getting down to roll. She felt the impaction with a rectal examination and tubed him which involved inserting a tube up his nostril and down into his stomach where warm water and paraffin were pumped in to try and soften and remove the blockage.

We longed for several days for him to pass droppings to show his system had cleared out and the vet visited each day to tube him.. Eventually he was taken to the equine hospital for surgery to remove the blockage as tubing wasn't working.

This was an incredibly scary time for Joanne and myself. He was her baby and, although I had only loaned him for three months, I felt a real bond with him too. I waited by the phone for that call to say he had woken from surgery. He woke up ok which was such a relief but we were

told that he wouldn't be 'out of the woods' for at least a week. We visited him several times that week and could see he was uncomfortable and was not making the speedy recovery we hoped he would.
Unfortunately though there was too much irreparable damage to his intestines. He wouldn't eat or drink or pass droppings. He just stood there shifting his weight uncomfortably and looking like he was in so much pain, despite being on a drip and on pain killers. We knew at this point that his gut wasn't going to kick start and the vet said the cells in his intestine had started to die. The horrible decision every horse owner dreads was made to end his pain and put him to sleep.
It was an incredibly tough day for Joanne and myself to watch this beautiful five year old Spanish horse go to waste. Colic is nasty. It can occur when least expected and kill a perfectly healthy young horse. Poor Dixey fought till the very end but it was his time.

After Dixey, my first real adulthood horse responsibility, I felt a sick, empty feeling. Part of my life was missing. That horse-shaped hole was back in my heart again! I was at a loose end and didn't know what to do with my spare time not having anything to care for. I managed to tolerate the feeling for a few months but it just got too much. I had to have my own horse! By no means a replacement for Dixey but another horse that I could care for and spend all my time with. I had so much love to give to another animal.
I was offered another loan horse on that same yard. A Clydesdale mare who was beautiful and kind and needed a friend for a couple of days a week. I took her on although I felt guilty as Dixey had only just gone but I needed to fill that hole in my heart.
As much as I loved that mare we just didn't connect. I'm not sure why. Maybe I just wasn't ready to let go of Dixey or maybe it was because I had my heart set on a Spanish horse. Either way I chose to give her up.
It was time that I looked for my own horse. A horse that was all mine and so the search began. Of course that search was for a Spanish horse! I looked through many adverts. They were all completely out of my price range or were too far away but I kept searching. I would eventually find the right one. The one who will not only fill that hole in my heart but cause my heart to explode with unquestionable love for it, lifting me to

the heavens where my dreams lie, to bring my dreams back to planet Earth.

The very early years!

Dixey

Joanne and her gorgeous Dixey the day before we lost him

The Soul and Spirit Unite

It was proving difficult to find my new friend as Spanish horses were not that common in the UK at the time. I eventually found a lovely grey gelding down in Sussex that was cheap and to be sold as a project horse. He was absolutely stunning with that dreamy long mane you would expect with an Andalusian. I made a phone call to arrange to go and view him. It would be an eight hour round trip but would be worth it if he was right for me. The following day though I got a call back to say he had been sold. I guess it wasn't meant to be.

I then found a horse named Dillon on a horse website and rang up to ask a little more about him. He was a six year old Andalusian stallion, 15.2hh, ride and drive. His photo was stunning although he looked a little chunkier than the Spanish horses I had seen. He had previously been used as a driving horse for weddings but was up for sale as they couldn't find a matching pair for him. I decided to drive all the way to Shropshire to view him the same day as his owner said he already had someone interested in him. I dragged my boyfriend there with me. He was not really into horses but I wanted someone there with me.

We arrived there and the horse was in a dirty old barn that had seen better days. He had a really heavy winter coat and was in rather poor condition. He was covered in mud and stable stains and had a nasty cough - hardly looked like the horse in the photo! He looked more like a woolley pony than an Andalusian. You could see the Spanish in his eyes though, in his innocent, gentle gaze. My excitement at viewing him had given way to sadness. It wasn't right to see a horse like this. Not what I would call acceptable.

His owner said he had mostly been driven in the past but was broken to ride. He had only had him about three months and he had come from a dealer previously. I had a ride on him and he pretty much refused to move. It didn't help that he was suffering from this cough. I eventually managed to get an unbalanced canter in one of the fields after struggling to get a walk and trot out on the road. I knew in the back of my mind that I should walk away. This wasn't my dream horse. He wasn't the stunning, prancing beast that I really wanted and he was clearly ill with the cough but I was very drawn to him. This is why you should always take a knowledgeable, sensible horse person with you when you go and view a horse!

We went into the owner's house to discuss him and I then discovered he wasn't papered and carried a Belgian passport with very little information on it. Just his name and chip number. Just another thing that meant I should walk away. There was a name of a previous owner in Belgium but who knows how long ago that was. This meant that he could have been in many homes and ownership was never transferred. The price he was asking for this horse was way too much. There was something about Dillon though, something beyond the woolly coat, the grass belly and serious lack of topline that drew me to him. I saw him as an overpriced project horse but there was something else about him. I handed over a deposit.

Preparations took place at the riding school in Carrington to get ready for the arrival of my new horse. My excitement was indescribable! Those childhood dreams once again becoming reality but this time he was all mine! His stable was located in a small block of two. The other stable belonged to my new friend Sarah who had a lovely chestnut Thoroughbred mare named Dolly. She would be his new neighbour and Sarah would remain my friend for life. Sarah had just started working at the yard and was as excited as me to see my new boy.

Dillon, now named Spirit, arrived on 2nd December 2009 in his very sorry state and castrated as requested. Stallions weren't allowed on the yard where he was to be kept. For weeks while waiting for him to be vetted, waiting for him to get over his cough and waiting for the castration I was writing lists of possible names for him. I wanted to choose my own name for him. He needed something else, something more majestic. The name Spirit, which to me meant a higher being, something to connect with and feel in your soul, was decided the day before he arrived despite the fact that I had heard that it was bad luck to change a horse's name. I know that now!

I remember the day clearly. As he was led off the horsebox people looked at him, probably wondering what possessed me to buy such a horse. Unfortunately though, as he was castrated as a mature stallion there were immediate complications in the form of infections. One after the other. As a new horse owner I learned very quickly about infections and how to deal with them! Not the ideal thing to happen for a first time horse owner!

Life was good, although a little scary with this massive responsibility. At the grand age of 28 I finally had my own horse. It was a dream come true! Something I had waited for all of my life. I had Spirit re-passported with the British Association for the Purebred Spanish Horse. As I had no breeding information on him and no parentage he was registered as a Spanish 'type'. Not quite the purebred I dreamed of but I loved him all the same and he was mine!

That winter was the coldest and snowiest we had experienced in many years. The only turnout we had at the yard for the winter was a tiny muddy paddock at the end of the yard that we could use for an hour a day. Being a keen photographer and absolutely loving my new horse, Sarah and I decided to put Spirit and Dolly out together in the paddock in the deep snow. It was amazing watching them both gallop and leap about. Spirit would shovel the snow with his nose, snort then bolt off. I got some fabulous photos of them both. What a fab day! Despite getting my car stuck in the snow and having to dig it out it was all worth it to see them both froliking about in the snow, Spirit in his shiny new turnout rug enjoying freedom and his new friend.

I clipped Spirit for the first time that winter which was an experience. A task that took several hours as he looked similar to a polar bear. He was a fidget and really didn't appreciate what I was doing but it had to be done. He was covered in scabs from what looked like rain scald. They looked sore so it gave me a chance to treat them. Being clipped also showed just how underweight and under muscled he was. Poor lad. At least he was safe now and I would give him the best life possible.

As the months passed, Spirit put on some weight. This started turning into muscle and he gradually turned into that beautiful swan that I saw beyond all that hair that day in Shropshire. It was no plain sailing though. He obviously felt better as he had become bolshy and nippy. He had very little respect for me. It appeared he had never been schooled, literally just sat on. He wouldn't tolerate the company of other horses and was completely unsocialised from his previous life as a stallion. He would kick out at anything, rear and drag me about the yard. Now it made sense why they couldn't find a matching pair to drive him with. He attacked everything. He seemed ok with Dolly though. They would scrap occasionally but he really liked her.

I was feeling a little out of my depth with him. I wanted a project horse but not necessarily something this green. He bucked often which started to throw my confidence. I never felt like he was trying to get me off but it was unnerving and I couldn't figure out why he was doing it.

Reality was kicking in and I was struggling with time and money and he had turned out to be a difficult horse, often dangerous. I even considered selling him at one point. I was constantly being told he was a man's horse, that he was too much for me, that he would seriously injure me. It was Sarah that stuck with me and encouraged me to keep going and prove them all wrong. So I did. I had waited all my life for this and I wasn't giving up so easily. I made a commitment to Spirit when I bought him that he would be in a forever home.

This is where Helen came into my life. Someone who has now become a very good friend and has always been there for me. I had decided to part loan Spirit to help with costs and schooling. I didn't know Helen beforehand but she was pointed in my direction by one of the instructors at the yard. She had moved up to Manchester from Hampshire to do a nursing degree and she had booked a lesson at the riding school to get her horsey fix. She put the word out that she was looking for a part loan and that's how she found Spirit. We hit it off straight away and she absolutely adored Spirit. He seemed to like her too! The three of us connected and I knew things would be great for Spirit's future.

Between us we turned Spirit's life around. We schooled him from scratch. We lunged, long reined and rode him and even taught him to bow. It was a rocky road but we really progressed with him. He still had stallion attitude but he had the most amazing, entertaining personality to go with it. We attended local shows and discovered his love for jumping. All in all we both had an amazing time with him although, as expected, it had its ups and downs. He became better in the company of other horses although we still had a few incidents of him attacking others. He became more respectful of Helen and myself and became much easier and safer to handle. We still had to lead him in a chifney though as he would just go off in whichever direction he wanted!

We discovered he loved to destroy things... He cracked open an 'indestructible' treat ball by simply kicking it at the wall! He figured out that it would be a much quicker way to get the treats out than rolling it around with his nose all day. He would deal with small holed haynets simply by making the holes larger with his teeth. He was so greedy he would eat whatever was available to him. We went through an incredible amount of feed buckets as they only lasted a few minutes with him. The best memory I have is the 'bucket of happiness'. It sounds a little odd but this bucket still sits in my room at home on display. This came about because Sarah was having a rubbish day working at the yard and when she came round past my stable I showed her Spirit's latest bucket death. A lovely purple feed bucket that he had neatly folded then squashed the life out of. We both burst out laughing and we named it the 'bucket of happiness'! It brings a smile to my face everytime I look at it. That's one dead bucket I will never throw away.

There are plenty of fun memories and some pretty scary ones too. How he didn't seriously injure us or kill us I will never know but somehow our bond became so strong I felt safe with him. His reputation at the yard with other horses was not good though despite his behaviour improving and in the summer he was banned from all day turnout with the others. He still had the stallion trait of biting the withers of other horses so he had to go out on his own in the winter paddock, sometimes with Dolly. We were lucky to have miles and miles of off road hacking attached to the farm. Great for building up fitness and muscle. I discovered that Spirit wasn't all that happy on the roads especially with big scary trucks but he improved over time. There was one hack that I will never forget while we were out with Sarah and Dolly. The ground was rather wet from weeks of rain but that never put us off. We were quite happily riding along one of the paths through the trees when we hit a really muddy spot. We had ridden over this patch many times in the past and never had a problem but due to the rain we were in for a surprise.

Spirit walked on into the mud. I expected he would probably sink to the fetlocks but was shocked when his legs just disappeared and he sank down to his belly! He seemed stuck there. My feet, still in the stirrups, were resting on the ground. He surged up a couple of times but he was well and truly stuck. It was then that I realised it might be a fire brigade job to free him! Sarah looked on thinking the same as me that he would need to be rescued.

I decided the best thing to do was to get off so he had a better chance of pulling himself out. I took my right foot out of the stirrup and swung it over his back and without warning he made another surge for freedom. My left foot was still in the stirrup so his movement flung me backwards and as he freed himself I was hanging off his side from the stirrup with my back lay flat in the mud! When I realised neither Spirit or myself were hurt I laughed. Poor Sarah didn't know what to do but then started laughing when I did. Thank God Spirit always thought about food first as he stood still and ate the nearby grass. He could so easily have run off with me attached to his side!

I learnt a valuable lesson from this. Always take both feet out of the stirrups!!!!! We got the horses home and gave Spirit a bath and thankfully he had escaped uninjured. We were very lucky that day. Just another one of our memorable adventures.

Spirit when I viewed him in Shropshire

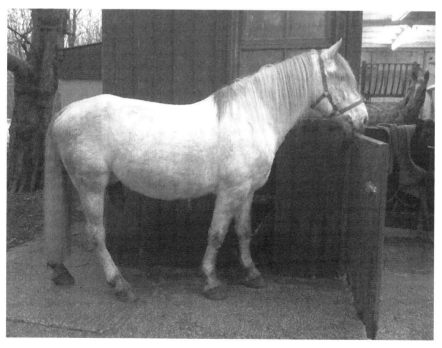

Spirit in his new home

Spirit and Dolly

Dolly, Sarah, her daughter Emily

Stress Testing the Relationship

It was one summer's day that I went into Spirit's stable and something wasn't quite right. Spirit didn't greet me as he normally would, demanding food. He just stood in his stable with his head low in the corner and was unresponsive. As a still relatively new horse owner this terrified me. My gut feeling said to get the vet despite people telling me that I worry too much and that there was nothing wrong with him. I'm so glad I did. Blood tests showed he was in the early stages of liver disease, most likely from ragwort poisoning. The liver wasn't functioning properly and was at risk of failing completely.

I was worried sick. I knew we were at risk of losing him which made me feel ill. My baby, my special horse that I had waited so long for was finally here in my life and I may lose him. I remember giving Helen the news and crying on her shoulder. I had no experience dealing with this illness and knew very little about it. The vet said there was a chance he wouldn't get through it but there were a few treatments we could try. Milk thistle was one thing to try so I managed to find some on Ebay and started it in his feed as soon as possible.

It was touch and go for a while as we monitored him and waited to see if the treatment was working. If it didn't work it meant his liver was too far gone and he would have to be put to sleep. Symptoms of liver disease don't normally appear until it's too late.

As a natural worrier I was thinking I was going to lose my precious boy that I had waited my whole life for and who's life I had turned around and made better. He certainly didn't deserve this illness and neither did I.

He had some time off and was on complete box rest so we could monitor his food and water intake. He had regular blood tests every few weeks to keep an eye on his liver function. A combination of antibiotics, the milk thistle and tons of tlc helped him pull through and months later his liver function was back to normal. He was a very lucky boy! All this meant a huge step back in his education though and he lost muscle tone which took a long time to get back. It was a real scare and definitely a learning curve for me.

Despite not being able to ride, Helen stuck with us. Spirit meant as much to her as he did to me. It was great to have her support at such a difficult time.

Soon after this we decided to move him to a different yard where there was more turnout and better socialisation for him. It was only down the road so wasn't such a major move but it meant that Spirit could be out all day and night which was better for him. Sarah had decided to move Dolly too as she and Spirit had become good friends. They were funny together, like a love hate relationship. I'm sure Dolly taught him a lot of life lessons! They would be able to go out in the field together. I wondered if Spirit had been taken from his mum before he was ready and then perhaps isolated as a stallion rather than being allowed to grow up and learn to be a horse. I think Dolly was like a mum to him, teaching him all the things he should have learnt as a youngster.

We loved the new yard. Helen, Sarah, myself and our horses settled well and were happy with the facilities and hacking. Knowing that Spirit loved to jump we were excited that there were two jumping paddocks there. We could really bring him on and start jumping competitions and dressage.

Unfortunately though one vet bill and insurance claim led to another. The happiness at the new yard was very short lived. I received a phone call from the yard owner one morning. I couldn't answer as I was driving to the farm but I knew it was something bad for him to be ringing me. Just a few minutes later I pulled into the yard car park to see three men standing outside Spirit's stable. One of them was the yard owner who, as I got out of my car, told me not to panic but Spirit had had an accident. Naturally I did panic and went into the stable to find him standing there holding his right hind leg awkwardly with blood dripping from high up inside his leg all the way down to his hoof. His leg had already ballooned from the stifle down to the fetlock.

I was told he was found with his leg stuck over the partition wall that separated his stable from the mares stable next door. The partition was about four foot high of solid wood with mesh at the top. It took the three of them to lift him back over. They had no idea how long he had been stuck there but he was apparently really calm and allowed himself to be rescued. I immediately thought he had broken the leg. From the stifle down it was limp. He had sweated up and was clearly in a lot of pain. How could this be happening? He gets over the liver disease but now he could be put down with a broken leg!

Once again I called the vet who rushed out to see him. Once cleaned up it didn't look quite as bad as it had originally and he was starting to put a little weight on it. However, his skin was severely damaged from high up near his sheath down to his hock and beyond where all his weight had been resting on the wall. Mid way up his thigh it was scraped down to bare muscle.

The wound had to be cleaned, cold hosed, creamed and packed twice a day and he narrowly escaped needing a skin graft. It looked awful and unfortunately he could reach it so he was forever biting at it. He needed a plastic cone like dogs have after surgery but they don't make them horse size! It was an extremely long healing process and not for the squeamish! Helen was great at it being a trainee nurse but I struggled a bit, especially packing the deep parts of the wound with gauze. It had to be done though so the wound would heal from the inside out. Keeping the flies away was the hard part as we were going into summer. We smothered fly repellent gel around the wound but that didn't work. We had to keep him in as much as possible on the hot and sunny days but that wasn't great for him as the fluid would keep building up without him moving about. The flies were so bad they managed to get in the wound and lay eggs despite our best efforts! The vet had to come back and strip the scabs back and clean out all of the eggs. This was a horrible and messy thing to watch but was necessary.

It took several months before the wound finally closed up and the hair grew back leaving a 6 inch black scar on the inside of that right hind leg. Little did we know that the scar would be very important in the future.

Spirit was soon back in work and we continued to enjoy our time with him. Jumping and hacking and generally having fun with Sarah and Dolly. We spent the summer going to shows, having horsey photo shoots, bathing days, long summer hacks and just relaxing, watching our horses in the field. Good times that I miss so much. Life was so good back then and I would give anything to re-live those days.

The more we realised that Spirit could jump the more we wanted to go out and about with him. We had the opportunity to go to Kelsall cross country course and with Helen being the braver rider she would take him round the farm ride there and see what he was like over solid jumps. Solid jumps terrified me! It was an interesting day as it was the first time I had tried to load Spirit into a horsebox. Fortunately Dolly loaded easily but Spirit was having none of it. It took us two hours to get him on board with lunge lines and food but eventually we were ready for the off. Just another one of his issues we would need to work on.

We had such a great time. We took turns riding, Helen trying the big jumps and me jumping the tiny logs. It was so good to see Spirit so happy, fit and healthy despite the terrible time we had in the past with his health. He loved the water and Kelsall has a wonderful water complex with jumps into and out of the water. He was a little cautious at first but was quite happily jumping in once he was confident. Love my little jumping horse.

A sad time came not so long after. We knew it was going to happen but it just came round so fast. Helen had to leave and go back to her hometown of Liphook in Hampshire. She had completed the nursing degree she had come up to Manchester for. She had graduated, and with the lack of jobs in the Manchester area she was forced to return home. It was an emotional time as she had bonded with Spirit as much as I had. She contributed to Spirit's training hugely and I knew things wouldn't be the same without her. We had become great, lifelong friends. I could see that Spirit missed her. He became quiet and rather withdrawn for a while.

Sarah, Helen and myself had such a great time together with our horses and the fact that Helen had to go home hit all of us. Things would never be the same.

I was left in that same situation again with no money or time so the hunt began for another sharer for Spirit. This is where Sophie came along. I found her through an advert on a horse sale website. Sophie clicked with spirit especially as they both loved jumping and it was agreed that she would look after him a few days a week like Helen did. We continued Spirit's schooling and he was taken to a few more local competitions. Life was good again.

Spirit's leg after the accident.

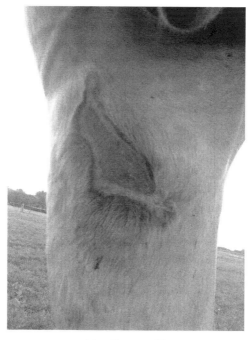

Healing well!

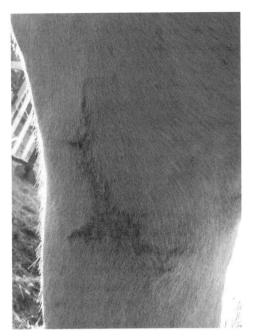

The final scar. A fabulous identifying mark.

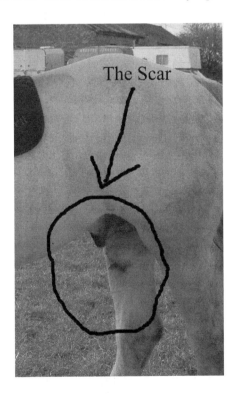

Helen and Spirit at Kelsall

Before and after of Spirit

From Better to Worse

It was the beginning of summer 2011 when the horses on the farm were allowed out in the field 24/7. It was the time of the year we all would look forward to. It was more natural for the horses to be out all the time and much cheaper for us to keep them. Spirit, now socially accepted, loved his time in the field where he could run with his friends and eat as much as he wanted. It made me so happy to see him 'being a horse', living life like a horse should. Such a contrast to the day I saw him in his sorry state in that barn in Shropshire. But it was short lived. The worst day of my life was about to begin.

I was at work teaching a riding lesson when I received the dreaded phone call. My phone kept ringing as I was teaching and I had to keep ignoring it as the rules were no mobile phone calls during lessons. As it rang 3 or 4 times i knew there was a problem. Then one of the other girls at the riding school came to the fence and told me she had also had the call and I urgently needed to answer my phone. I didn't realise the urgency at the time and told the girl I couldn't answer and could she find out what the problem was. I would call back after the lesson. She came back to me a few minutes later saying I had to answer my phone. Spirit wasn't in the field.

Sophie had gone down to ride him, went out to the field to bring him in and she couldn't find him. It was a 38 acre field with just 12 horses in it with plenty of dips and undulations for a horse to temporarily disappear in. The river Mersey ran through it. My immediate thought was that he was hiding behind a bush or had got down into the river. Either way my heart was doing back flips.

I got someone to cover the rest of the lesson and drove as fast as I could down the road to the farm. We walked the perimeter of the field three times, my heart pounding, checking the river, the fences, the ditches, constantly casting an eye over the whole area. I was trying to establish when he was last seen. Another horse owner confirmed that he was in the field at 9pm the night before when she did a last check on them all. Another owner said he wasn't in the field at 7am that morning, the morning of the 9th May. She thought nothing of it as one of us could have taken him out somewhere. It wasn't unusual for a horse to not be in the field as owners rode at different times of the day.

The panic was rising as I realised he had actually disappeared without a trace. While out in the field I called the police and told several friends who within minutes were out in the field helping us look. I felt sick. It wouldn't be the first time a horse had fallen into the river from that field and drowned. We checked all the banks for disturbance but there was nothing. More people gathered to help with the search and set out in their cars looking in case he had simply escaped. All the local farms were contacted and Irlam locks, where the river leads to, was checked in case he was washed up there.

While still out in the field I posted on Facebook that Spirit was missing. Social media was an important tool in this situation. A very fast way to spread the word. On closer inspection of the fencing by the road it seemed it had been tampered with. I climbed over to find Spirit sized hoof prints on the other side. It was then that we came to the conclusion that he had been stolen.

I don't know how I stayed so calm. I mean, I was panicking but not hysterical or crying. Adrenaline is such an amazing thing! While the growing search party was out I waited at the farm for the police to arrive. They took my statement then came out to the field to look at the fencing. It was then that they gave me a crime reference number. It was now officially a theft.

I asked for a helicopter to go out and look for him, an absurd request in retrospect, but they said all they could do is send out a car to check nearby. They told me a stolen horse is treated no differently to a stolen wallet or mobile phone. They used to hang people for horse theft! I couldn't believe it. This was my baby. This horse was my whole life. How could the police refer to my horse, my child, my dream, my SPIRIT as a mere inanimate object? I felt so angry at this. The police were there to help me surely, not just pass this off as minor incident.

Later that evening everyone had gathered back at the yard tired and fruitless. He was obviously long gone. There was no CCTV in the area to check and there hadn't been a single sighting. They must have taken him in the night. It confused me as he was difficult to load. How did they take him away? If they had led him somewhere someone would have seen him with it being a built up area. If they had tried to load him there would have been lots of noise and commotion. It was to remain a mystery.

The decision was made to go home and rest as Spirit was obviously not going to be found that day. Everyone was so supportive and looked after me. Only when I was on my own in my car driving out of the farm gates I completely lost it and sobbed my heart out all the way home. Not the best idea to be in such a state while driving down the M60 at night! It had finally sunk in that some sick and twisted person had taken my beloved horse, my boy. Was this really happening? Surely this only happens to other people. My emotions were so mixed. One minute I was seething with anger at the person who took him, the next I was feeling like my heart had been ripped out.

As soon as I got home I figured the best way to spread the word was to go down the social networking route. I created a group on Facebook called 'Spirit stolen, please help find him'. I posted a full description, photos and the story so far and was amazed that I got 100 members that evening. Word had to be spread. We had to stop the thieves in their tracks, make Spirit too hot to handle. With my team of friends and group members we contacted vets, farriers, slaughterhouses, ports and airports across the country. The most important thing at that stage was to stop them taking him out of the country.

I barely slept that night if at all. I was on the group most of the night spreading the word and replying to the hundreds of messages asking about Spirit. The members mounted up. 200, 300, 400. The support was overwhelming and I was starting to feel I would have him home in a couple of days, hoping that he would be dumped somewhere and found by a passer by.

The next day I went back out to the farm for another walk around the field although I knew there really wasn't much point. I decided I was more use at home at my computer running the Facebook group. As I gathered members in the group word spread fast. My phone did not stop. Concerned friends and relatives wanted to offer their support. I found out the next horse auction in the area was Beeston in just three days so myself and a few friends decided we needed to be there as it seemed likely that he could be taken there for a quick sale.

We went and checked out all the horseboxes at the sales as we thought he probably wouldn't go through the auction ring as it would raise suspicions. There was no sign of him.

While we were there I recieved a phone call from a member of the Facebook group saying she had been contacted by a meat man who had been offered Spirit for meat. At this early stage of the search I thought this was going to be the moment I would find out where he was and we could be reunited. I remember being in tears on the phone with absolute joy that the nightmare was going to come to an end. It all seemed rather odd to me though and it didn't feel quite right the more I thought about it. Why had I not received that phone call directly from the meat man? Who was this woman and how did she get involved? I got in touch with the meat man and he explained that he had been offered Spirit for meat but thought he was too good for that then noticed that he met the description of my missing horse. I was in pieces on the phone to him and got sucked in by it all. He said he could buy the horse so he was safe and then I could buy him back off him. Being in the fragile state I was in, I wasn't thinking very clearly. I had to find the money. As time went on though and after many phone calls the man wasn't able to get me any photos of the horse or any real confirmation that it was him. He just swore that it was.

I knew it was all a bit dodgy when he insisted that I don't get the police involved. He wasn't clear as to why. He just said he wanted to deal with me directly. So it started out that he would buy the horse and I would give him the cash when I picked him up. Then he changed his mind and wanted cash first before I saw the horse. During all of this, which was going on now over several days, my friends and I headed on the long drive down to Gloucester to a horse fair in Stow on the Wold.

It was an odd experience at the horse fair, we stuck out like a sore thumb as it was full of travellers. There was a lot of horse trading going on and my eyes were on stalks looking out for Spirit, all the time being harassed by the meat man on my mobile phone who by now I knew was fake. He was now getting desperate and menacing and was giving me time deadlines to get the money from me. He had decided he wanted it in his bank account before I had even seen the horse.

Despite his request I reported the meat man to the police saying I was being harassed and that he claimed to know where my horse was.

Having to deal with all of this while searching a horse fair in an unfamiliar part of the country was really killing me. I was so grateful to have my friends there supporting me. The police took the meat man's name and investigated him. He denied all knowledge to the police which confirmed it a hoax. It made me sick that someone could do that to me when I was already suffering from a great loss.

Thankfully not all of our communication had been through phone calls. Lots had been through text message so I sent the police all of the texts that had become progressively abusive. They said they would consider a case for pressing charges of harassment.

It was a long and sad drive home from that horse fair. No sign of my beautiful boy and the complete horror of dealing with the hoax caller really took its toll.

Weeks passed, every day becoming more and more painful. Part of me was missing Spirit badly and part was sick with worry as to whether he was being looked after or if he was even alive. I felt that part of my soul had been taken along with Spirit that day. There was a huge hole left in my heart that only he could fill. I also felt immense anger at those who took him. I had absolutely no idea who. I didn't have any enemies as far as I knew. Who would do this to me? It was sickening that there were people out there that would just take something so precious. They obviously never understood the bond that someone could have with a horse and that they become part of you. They become family. And what made it even worse is that I had worked so hard and waited so long to finally have a horse of my own and they just took him. I only had 18 months with him. Helen and I turned him around and made him something special and now he was gone. They would probably never appreciate him or bond with him like I did. Those dreams I had as a child had come true but were now turning into a horrible nightmare.

These weeks turned into months but as the pain grew so did the group on Facebook. At this point we had a few thousand members. Spirit had now made it into two local papers and I had been on two local radio stations. Spirit had made it into three major national horse magazines too which was just what we needed. Group members were distributing posters across the country and the mission continued to inform vets, farriers, saddlers, auctions etc. Word was spreading fast and complete strangers were becoming friends.

Two of those strangers were Jill and Tracie. We became good friends in the virtual world of Facebook. Spirit had really captured their hearts and they were to play a massive part in the search for him. They became admin for the group and a huge campaign for Spirit's return got under way. They supported me every step of the way and spent so much time on the phone and out distributing posters, not only around their own areas but posting wads of posters out to other supporters across the country for them to distribute. They piled loads in financially which helped me hugely as I had no money from travelling the country to horse fairs and auctions etc.

Every day I would receive many, many messages and emails with pictures of grey horses that could be Spirit. These were either adverts of horses for sale or photos people had taken of horses they had seen out and about. Tracie and Jill had to take some of these messages and emails and deal with them for me as I was so overwhelmed by them all. It was so great to know that people really were out looking and not just supporting through Facebook.

I left my job at the riding school. I was so focused on the search for my boy that I lost all enthusiasm for my job. I was starting to lose my confidence with horses too. I suffered a nasty fall while taking a hack out with the riding school, landing on a fence and damaging my back, and on a separate occasion one of my clients had a bad fall and had to be airlifted to hospital. The first time I had ever experienced the air ambulance! That was the last straw for me. I no longer wanted to be an instructor.

I took a new job as a groom at another yard. Purely a livery yard where I could work with the horses but not be an instructor. I was welcomed there with open arms. Most of the people there already had heard about Spirit and were full of support. I was happy that I had found a place to settle working with horses as I needed that contact with them. It's a good form of therapy being around these amazing animals. I needed them in my life and with Spirit gone it was vital I kept in touch with the horse world.

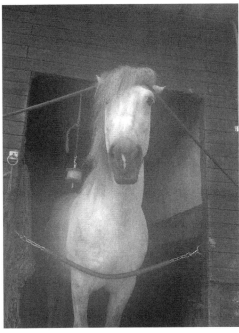

Emptiness Leads Me to Merlin

Towards the end of the summer I was trying to continue with life the best I could. The 'possible Spirit' messages were still coming through thick and fast which created mixed emotions. I was thrilled because the support was going strong and we would one day find him, yet sad as I had my hopes dashed with every message I was sent that wasn't him. I learned over time not to get my hopes up and started to become a bit numb to it.

I had planned to go to a large show for the purebred Spanish horse with my friend Joanne whom I shared Dixey with. My passion for Spanish horses was still there. It was going to be a fab weekend and a much needed get away for me. Accommodation was booked as the show was in Bedfordshire and I had booked time off at work. I was so excited to meet all the people on the Spanish scene.

I received an anonymous phone call the day before we were due to set off. A possible sighting of Spirit. The person was so sure it was him. She said that she had viewed the horse to buy, that he looked just like Spirit and that the passport she was shown looked fake. Based on that I called the local police with all the information I had been passed. The sighting was in Otley in West Yorkshire. The police got involved and I was told to have a horsebox on standby incase they found him. Fortunately the police woman dealing with it was horsey so knew what she was looking for. She knew the yard and would go in and investigate. Waiting for the phone call with the result of the search of this farm was almost painful. I was pretty sure this was it. I thought that my weekend at the show was cancelled. I couldn't possibly go away if Spirit was found. I would never want to leave him again.

The police called me back. No horse was found there matching his description. I cried. I was so sure. Was it another hoax or was it him and this lady spooked them which prompted them to hide him? I would never know. I thought it was all going to be over. So even without Spirit home, I still didn't feel like going to the show. It was such a huge disappointment. It seemed to be the closest we had been to getting him back. I just wanted to go home and hide away but despite all this I was encouraged to go anyway and try to clear my mind and have a good time.

And I did! It was amazing! The weather was perfect, beautiful surroundings, Spanish music playing and plenty of stunning Spanish horses. Definitely a mood lifter. I took so many photos, another real passion in my life. There I was introduced to a lady named Katie who had her own Spanish stud yard down south. She had heard about Spirit through Facebook and from others in the Spanish community.

She said she wanted to talk to me and was hoping I would come to the show so we could meet. What she said I was least expecting. She was offering to GIVE ME a five month old purebred Spanish colt! Could this be the start of my dreams becoming real again? They had felt so far away, away with my Spirit. My soul cruelly torn apart the day he was taken. Could this little colt have been sent to me by Spirit to ease the pain? She felt sorry for what I had been through with Spirit and felt she could offer me this colt. She explained that she wouldn't be able to sell him due to a deformity in his neck but wanted him to go to a good home where he would be treated well and completely spoilt. I was overwhelmed by this. To be given a purebred Spanish colt. A dream come true. MY dreams come true! I was immediately on the phone to Laura at the yard where I worked asking for a stable and luckily there was one free. I would just have to wait a little while longer for him to be weaned before I could collect him.

The rest of that weekend was pure bliss. The gorgeous sunshine and Spanish music continued. I met some amazing people and was even referred to as the 'famous Spirit lady' by the big names in the Spanish community. This was good. We were becoming well known which meant the word was spreading fast around the country. It was just a fabulous weekend.

So the preparations began to get ready for the foal arriving. I had to wait until winter for him to be weaned. I had a long wait considering it was only September. I went to visit Helen in Hampshire in October and together we took the trip to go and visit the foal. He was stunning. A near-perfect little dark bay colt. Perfectly put together apart from his neck deformity. He had been x-rayed at birth to find out what was wrong. His 1st cervical vertebrae was dislodged and had set to one side. I was told he could lead a normal life and that it would just be cosmetic. That didn't bother me. He would be my perfect little boy. It was fabulous meeting all of Katie's stallions including the foal's sire, the magnificent Milagros. Despite having a new horse entering my life I never let up on the search for Spirit. I was excited for him to come home and meet his foalie friend! The Facebook group just kept on growing as did the 'possible spirit' messages. Support was coming in from all over the world. People in America and Australia were sharing my posts about Spirit and although it was extremely unlikely that he had been taken that far away it felt good that people were thinking of him. It was only a matter of time until someone spotted him somewhere. He just had to be recognised eventually. I had heard stories of stolen horses reappearing after ten years and being reunited with their owners. That gave me hope!

The time came for my little foal to be weaned and transported to me. By then I had decided his name would be Merlin. I wanted a name that was mystical and magical to match his presence and beauty. I had prepped his stable with a nice deep bed, made a name plate for his door and bought a few tiny foal rugs. I was so excited and dreamt about our future together and all of the wonderful things that we could do and achieve. The excitement was often dampened by a sickening guilty feeling though. Could I cope with loving another horse? Would spirit know about this foal and how would he feel? I would never give up looking for him but when he returned would I manage to divide my time evenly between them? My emotions played havoc while waiting for Merlin to arrive. I wasn't sure whether to even have him or not. My friends and family were supportive though and helped me decided that I needed another horse in my life. Something to look after before I went mad!

So Merlin arrived. I planned to have the best behaved colt so that I could keep him entire. A perfect opportunity having him so young. We spent the first few weeks learning and having fun. Melin learnt to wear a halter, rugs and surcingle. He learnt to play with a football, lead calmly by my side and had his feet picked up every day. He was growing to be a stunning boy. Sarah had followed me to Laura's yard with Dolly. There was a change in her behaviour when Spirit was taken and she seemed to really miss him. I truly believe that horses feel emotions of loss, grief, joy etc. I believe she was grieving for his loss. I wondered if she had all the answers as she was in the field the day he was taken. She would have seen who took him and how they did it but she could never tell us.

We introduced her to Merlin and she took him under her wing and treated him like her own baby.

During this time the search for Spirit continued. I wasn't going to let Merlin distract me from the search. We were now up to 7000 members on the facebook group. The hardest thing was to get more media attention. We had to keep spreading the word across the UK and beyond. It was great at first getting him in a few newspapers and magazines but we were struggling with anything else. Crimewatch and BBC showed an interest but never followed it through. Petitions were started on the internet to get more media attention. Unfortunately at this point though it was becoming old news and it has harder to get anyone interested in covering the story. Horse theft was a lot more common than I initially thought and it destroys people's lives. I wanted to tell the world and make people aware.

It was early in the new year. I wanted this to be my year. To watch Merlin grow and for Spirit to come home. Merlin was growing and with it grew the problem in his neck. I could see as time passed that he was struggling to get his head down to graze, more than the average foal would. The deformity was more obvious and it made his neck rigid. I couldn't see how he would ever be ridden as flexing at the poll was virtually impossible. I was concerned that he may be in pain. Maybe not severe pain as he was just so docile but maybe just a dull and constant headache. I decided to have him x-rayed again to check how he was developing as he was growing all the time. But with these x-rays brought bad news. The problem had become worse as he grew. His 1st cervical vertebrae was now growing into his skull. This had shortened his already short and compact neck by about 4 inches. Due to this he could probably never be ridden and could end up in incredible pain especially if the spinal cord became pinched. Grazing would always be an issue for him as his neck was just not long enough for him to reach the grass without dramatically splaying his front legs.

At just seven months old poor baby Merlin was peacefully put to sleep with Sarah and I by his side at the equine hospital. A truly devastating moment in my life and a very difficult decision to make. This further opened up the gaping wound of losing Spirit. Another loss, more emptiness. I felt useless and hopeless and once again, horseless.

Apart from his neck he just looked so happy and healthy and perfect. It seemed wrong to end his life when he didn't look ill but I knew it would be for the best long term. The vet said we could leave it months, even years and he may be ok but there was always the risk of him damaging his spinal cord and we couldn't tell if he was experiencing chronic pain. It had to be done there and then. I couldn't leave it, bond with him like I did with Spirit and then have a 95% chance of having to have him put to sleep years down the line. I couldn't believe my luck with horses. First losing Dixey then Spirit being stolen and now my poor little boy Merlin, taken from me at such an early age.

I had him cremated so I could always have him in my home. We had such a bond even in the short amount of time we had spent together. I was glad to have his ashes. At least I would always have a piece of him unlike Spirit. I didn't have any part of him, just a small amount of tangled mane in a brush.

I spoke to Katie. I felt she ought to know since he was a gift from her. She was gutted but more sorry than anything and she felt bad for putting me through it all. I cried so much for that little boy. I was beating myself up wondering if I had done the right thing. Maybe I should have given him a chance. What if he wasn't in pain and would have had a pain free life? But every time I thought like that I referred back to the x-rays and the problem was obvious. It was without doubt the right thing to do. It would have been selfish on my part to keep him alive.

So life went on. Horseless again and still no word on Spirit. The days and weeks became increasingly difficult. I became very down and depressed. Every day at work I had to be around Merlin's stable and it was so painful. Things started to go quiet on the Spirit group and I wondered if I should leave the world of horses. I felt every horse I would have I would lose. Several people had tried to encourage me to stop looking for Spirit and to move on and that dwelling on it was making me ill. Merlin's departure was almost confirmation that my life with horses was over.

There was no giving up though. Jill and Tracie helped step up the search for Spirit and were constantly there supporting me and sharing kind words. It was exhausting. It was a full time job and more keeping on top of messages and maintaining the Facebook group. The hoaxes didn't stop. I thought there would be a lot more than there were but I would often get prank calls and people claiming to have Spirit which all turned out to be people having some sick sort of laugh! As if the trauma of losing him in the first place wasn't enough. Some people just weren't right in the head.

My special little Merlin

Missing my Spirit

Spirit and Dolly. She misses him

Milagros

Horses horses horses! I just had to have one in my life! So I decided to contact Katie and see if she had any other foals up for sale that I could consider. Unfortunately she didn't but she would consider letting me have something on loan with a view to buy. I couldn't believe it when she offered me Milagros, Merlin's sire, for loan. A stunning 15.2hh purebred Spanish stallion of Carthusian breeding. He was a beautiful dark bay, almost black in some lights. I was so happy that she was willing to send him to me on loan so I could have him on a three year payment plan. A Spanish stallion! The horse of my dreams!

So the plans were put in place to have him vetted and get contracts sorted. I arranged to hire a horse box so I could go and pick him up from the stud. I was so excited! This would be my chance to really get into dressage and do some Spanish showing. So the day finally came for me to drive down south. Also my first time driving a horsebox. It was about a four hour drive down there but worth every minute of it as when we got there Milagros was standing there all shiny and beautiful with his mane long and flowing, ready to come home with me.

The first few weeks were full of mixed emotions for me. Milagros settled really well and with his exceptional manners he was quickly accepted on the yard. There was a bit of concern by the other people on the yard as he was a stallion but he soon proved himself to be perfectly behaved and very gentle although vocal. Only when he wanted food though! I on the other hand found it difficult. I felt guilty having him as the search for Spirit seemed to go on the back burner. Again, like Merlin, he was no means a replacement for Spirit but I found it difficult to connect and bond with him.

Due to the guilt I gave the search for Spirit an extra push, setting up an event on Facebook for a mass share of his posters and pictures. I knew I couldn't afford two horses so if he was found I wouldn't cope financially. I didn't care though. I would find a way.

Riding Milagros for the first time was heavenly. He moved so beautifully and for first time I was able to properly ride a canter half pass. He never put a foot wrong and was an absolute dream to ride. I felt so excited for the future with him.

But in true Lisa style it was never to be straightforward. I had only had Milagros two months when I started noticing problems in his performance. He wasn't lame but he definitely wasn't quite right. On his near fore fetlock there was a slight swelling that had appeared. With him not being lame I went through the process of cold hosing to see if that would help it go down. It didnt. It only got worse so the vet was called. Again he was not lame for the vet but he explained that it may be a problem with the suspensory ligament branch as they don't always show lameness with an injury there.

Milagros had a trip to the local horse hospital for an ultrasound scan where he was sedated and had the injured area shaved then scanned. The scan showed quite a serious injury to the suspensory branch. There was a huge hole in it which had obviously been building up for some time. They think probably around six months. Suspensory injuries only really show up when they are really bad and by then it's often too late to repair it fully. The prognosis for Milagros wasn't good and the vet estimated around 18 months for a reasonable recovery. He would never jump or be allowed a flat out gallop again.

Fortunately he was insured so I asked that he had all the possible treatment available to him. One type of treatment was the platelet injection. This is where they take some of his blood and put it in a centrifugal system to filter out the healing red blood cells. They then inject this directly into the ligament to speed up healing. Its a expensive treatment but worth it. My beautiful boy came home with a bandage from his knee down to his hoof that had to stay on for a week to prevent infection to the injection site. Box rest started and a recovery programme was put into place.

It was a long, drawn out recovery involving many scans, regular shock wave treatments and building up strength and stretch in the scar tissue with short, in hand walks twice a day building up from five minutes to half an hour over six weeks. It took patience but Milagros was perfect and so well behaved every step of the way. I think he was just lapping up the attention! After the six weeks the vet said I could ride him again. Just half an hour each day hacking in walk on hard ground. Another six weeks of that before I could increase it to 45 mins a day. I was itching to get on with his schooling and get out and compete but his recovery was so much more important.

So finally Milagros was ready for full work. £5000 of vets bills later he was signed off as fit. At this point dressage wasn't going to happen. We had to go back to basics with his training to build up his strength and stamina. When I felt it was time I took him out to a few local shows to do foreign breeds classes which he did well in but that injury was always on my mind and I was afraid to push him too much.

I was so so happy when we were selected to ride as part as the Spanish team in the London New Year's Day parade. Milagros had proven himself to be completely bomb proof and looked fabulous in his Spanish tack so my friend Joanne and I took our horses down to London to take part in this amazing, huge event. Such an incredible experience! Can't get a better feeling than riding through the centre of London on my beautiful boy waving to the crowds, appearing on tv and then having photos taken at the gates of Buckingham Palace and at Horse Guards Parade. We did this two years in a row. So proud of my boy! It was an incredible experience and it felt so amazing riding him at such a huge event, showing him off to the world. A day I will never forget. Surely this was it now. We were on the road to good times.

I hoped that things would go smoothly from there but it wasn't to be. I noticed over a period of time that Milagros was becoming lethargic and was starting to develop an oedema on his belly. It was a pitting oedema which felt a bit like plasticine when you pressed into it. This was a buildup of fluid and it grew larger and larger each day. Once again the vet was called. He had blood tests done and a rectal examination. Both came back clean but the oedema was growing and spreading to his sheath making it hard for him to pee. It spread to his chest also. He was called in to the hospital once again for further tests. He stayed in there for two long weeks. He was scoped to check for ulcers but was clean. He had biopsies and scans and following an ultrasound on his belly I was contacted by the vet saying he had inflammation of the stomach and the small intestine and that more in depth blood tests showed a dangerous drop in blood protein. His body wasn't absorbing blood protein as it should have which was causing the oedema.

This was a worrying time. The vets found it all a bit of a mystery. There was no name for this condition and vets from different practices were consulted to ask their opinion but it was something unusual. Typical! So treating it was tricky as we didn't know what was causing it. So he was started on a course of steroids to try and reduce the inflammation in the intestine. Weeks passed and the oedema started to disappear. His blood results were returning to normal and things were starting to look more hopeful. The problem was, every time we tried to wean him off the steroids the oedema came back and the blood proteins dropped again. The vet advised me that due to this he would probably be on steroids for the rest of his life which could potentially shorten his lifespan and increases the risk of laminitis. I was absolutely gutted. He was only ten. Poor boy didn't deserve this! Once again I would think back to my younger years, wishing for my own horse but I never wished for this. I knew it would never be plain sailing with horses but this??? Neither Milagros nor myself deserved this!

Again I was really thankful for his insurance. Another £5000 claim maxed out plus the on going cost of steroids for the foreseeable future. But I would do whatever it took to keep my boy happy and comfortable.

So life went on once Milagros' condition had stabilized. We managed to do a few more shows but nothing at a high level. The threat of laminitis was real with the steroids so he was on a very strict, no sugar diet. I decided to move him to my friends yard up in Skelmersdale. Rebecca was my instructor and I felt that Milagros being on her yard where she could school him and give me lessons would be the best thing for him to progress. I loved it there and Milagros seemed much happier. I had to change farrier as it was too far for my other farrier to travel. Having had heart bars and wedges on to help the suspensory ligament injury to heal we felt it was time for them to come off and perhaps we could try him barefoot. The heart bars, although necessary for the suspensory, had contracted his heels badly and going barefoot temporarily would help them to open up and for him to grow more heel.

It was quite a traumatic process. I knew he would be in some discomfort while he adjusted so I bought him some hoof boots and he had a big bed in his stable. I didn't ride so that he could take his time with the transition under his own weight. He was crippled. My farrier reassured me that this would happen and to give it time.

I gave it time and he only got worse so I asked the farrier if he would put some standard shoes back on to make him comfortable again. The farrier said that he really shouldn't be getting worse and that there was an underlying problem. He suggested x-rays. So, back to the hospital he went for x-rays. Another insurance claim was opened. He had laminitis. This was the last thing i wanted to hear. The steroids that were keeping him alive were killing him with laminitis! Why? Why was this happening? The vet told me straight that it may be best to have him put to sleep if we can't get him off the steroid and sort his feet out. I was potentially going to lose this beautiful horse that I had so strongly bonded with over the past two and a half years. We had been through thick and thin together. The decision was made to put shoes back on and take him off the steroids to see if he could heal the bowel problem himself. The oedema came back but regular blood tests again showed that the protein levels didn't drop as much as they did previously. Over time the oedema started to disappear and like a miracle his system managed to regulate itself. I was so relieved as he could now start to recover from the laminitis.

So the slow process of the recovery began. No riding, strict diet, minimal turnout and a lot of bute to make him comfortable.

None of my horsey friends had the sort of bad luck I'd been experiencing over the last few years! I was so exasperated by all of this but the bond between horse and rider makes it worth soldiering on. For me, there was no question about simply keeping on 'keeping on'.

However, the stress of Milagros' illnesses and travelling over an hour each way to the yard every day was taking its toll. I made the decision to move Milagros back to Lymm where he was closer to home. There was no point having him at Rebecca's yard if we couldnt school him between us.

So back at the yard in Lymm Milagros' laminitis reached a point where we could ride again but we had to start from the beginning again to build up his strength and stamina. That was another £5000 insurance claim to get through the laminitis. We started lots of slow hacking and fortunately he stayed sound but needed heart bar shoes to keep him comfortable.

Over the years that I had Milagros my mum was paying in installments to buy him but she was forced to take early retirement for health reasons so the payments fell on me. I wasn't earning enough for this and was struggling just to cover insurance premiums and livery etc. Six months previous I had decided to take on a horse photography franchise, to reduce my hours at the yard and do what I loved, photography and being around horses. I felt this was a good route to go down as it was to be good money and meant I could keep up those payments for Milagros and give him the care and attention he needed. It was an exciting new venture and I had plenty of training and met lots of new people. I turned my very amateur photography into something special and I finally became professional. I loved it! Being self employed the income was unpredictable but I got off to a great start.

I took this line of work as a great opportunity to spread the word further about Spirit. It meant I was travelling the north west more which meant I had the chance to look out more for greys in fields, I went to lots of yards where I checked out every stable I could looking for my boy. Every photo shoot I did I mentioned Spirit to my clients. Some had heard of him, others hadn't but were happy to spread the word further for me. Maybe the photography would lead me to my beautiful Spirit one day.

During the set up of my new business I sustained a foot injury from slipping in the field. I didn't think much of it at first and I thought the pain would pass but it didn't. My foot is a story in itself but I ploughed on trying to make my new business work.

I had a reasonable first summer with the photography but didn't earn as much as expected. I was just keeping afloat with livery, farrier and insurance payments but I was missing the payments towards buying Milagros. This was the beginning of the end for me. My mum and step dad supported me and Milagros for months until we basically 'bled them dry' and they could no longer help me. Keeping Milagros was becoming impossible with the cost of expensive shoes and regular x-rays for his feet. Going into winter the photography business went to nothing. No income whatsoever and with my foot now confirmed as broken I could only manage to work one or two days at the yard putting up with severe pain. In February 2015 the absolutely heartbreaking decision was made to let Milagros go back to the stud down south and lose him completely. I could no longer afford him and my three year contract had come to an end for me to finish paying for him. I still owed over half of his value. There was no way I could find that money.

The day he was collected will haunt me forever. Saying goodbye to the horse I had bonded with so strongly, more than I had bonded with Spirit in effect, who had been a part of my life every single day for three years, who we had been through thick and thin together, it was just so traumatic. I sobbed like a little child when Katie arrived to take him. I buried my face in his mane and hugged him, telling him I was so sorry I had let him down, sorry that I had failed him. My mum, step dad and I all felt strongly that when you take on an animal it's for life and that it went 'against the grain' to send him back. I still can't get over it a year on. It hurts to just think about it and makes me feel sick to my stomach.

Was I not supposed to have horses? Is it my destiny to be horseless? I tried my absolute best for all the horses in my life but have lost them all. I didn't deserve this. So he went. I felt so empty inside. Clearing out his stable and the tack room was an incredibly difficult task and the tears flowed. I felt I had no heart or soul left as the loss of Milagros ripped out what little remained.

My drawing of Milagros

Horseless and Hopeless

Horseless life began. I missed Milagros so much it hurt and it brought back all the hurt from my other lost horses. I started to go under into a massive depression. I had no job because of my injured foot and no purpose in life. I missed going to the yard every day to care for Milagros. That had become a way of life for many years and the loss of that routine hurt like crazy. I longed more than ever for Spirit to return. I needed him so desperately. He was my therapist, the one thing that could make me feel better and give each day a purpose. Without a horse I had no need to get up in the morning.

Things went from bad to worse for me. The foot, the stupid bloody foot that kept bugging me, wouldn't get better. I had gone for scans and x-rays and had repeatedly been told to go away and rest as much as possible but rest didn't help. Business was failing too. Through the winter I had no work whatsoever from the photography franchise. It wasn't going to plan! Due to the lack of work I was unable to keep up the franchise payments and after a meeting with the franchisor, a mutual decision was made for me to leave the franchise. It was through no fault of my own, it was just simply because the work wasn't out there to sustain several branches of the franchise in the north west. It was never going to work. So this left me with working just one day a week at the yard which I was struggling with because of my foot.

I soon had to give up that one day and that's when I hit absolute rock bottom. What was my life? Why was I here? I wasn't achieving anything, I was unemployed with not a penny to my name, in serious debt to my parents and a broken foot that the hospital was in no hurry to do anything about. I had lost far too many horses and I wondered if I had been cursed. Had I done something really bad and this was karma coming around to bite me on the arse? Horses were my whole life, I cared for them deep within my heart so why was I being denied one? There were some very dark moments when I felt I couldn't go on and considered ending it all. Spirit was probably happy in his home. He probably didn't miss me any more. After all he probably just lives in the moment and if he has food he is happy. I felt I had nothing left to give in this life. I didn't want to wake up in the morning as being awake hurt my brain and my emotions. Only my family and friends kept me going. I couldn't do that to them.

Through the depression I tried to relaunch the Spirit campaign and get more interest and attention. People said to me that Milagros had to go to make way for Spirit's return but that never came. The relaunch prompted people to come forward to donate money for a reward for Spirit's return. Something I had been warned not to do by police as it would encourage hoax calls. Since I was getting these anyway I decided to accept the money and make new posters displaying the reward. £3000 in total. Money I could only dream of having and without these few individuals the reward would not have been possible. I do want to point out that this money is not in my possession. It is in the hands of the people who have donated.

I was starting to feel positive although trying not to get my hopes up. £3000 is a lot of money and Spirit probably wouldn't be worth that right now. Surely this was a big enough incentive for someone to come forward. The new posters were distributed, word was spread as usual on Facebook. But still no one came forward.

It all gave me renewed hope and I eagerly waited for the phone to ring but that call never came.

So here I am, still waiting. Waiting for that one phone call that reunites me with my beautiful Spirit. My time with horses has been filled with so much pleasure and I have learnt so much. As they say, 'better to have loved and lost than to never have loved at all'. That is so true. One day I will buy another horse when I am financially stable and my foot is fixed. I am currently waiting for surgery so when that is sorted then the only way is up. I am determined to have my beautiful Spanish stallion, my horse for life, and to get my Spirit home. Watch this space...

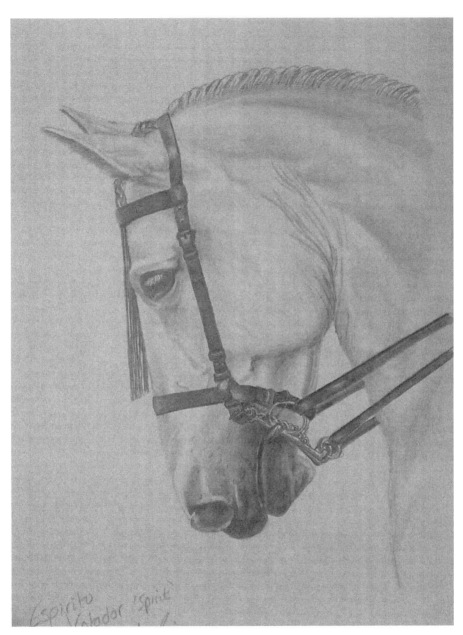
My drawing of Spirit

Final Word

The search for Spirit continues. It's been years but I will never give up. I am overwhelmed by the constant support from friends old and new who are still just as dedicated to find him as the day he went missing. So is there anything you can do to help? Yes! Keep spreading the word. Tell your farrier, your vet, saddle fitter, dentist etc. Print out some posters and put them in your local tack and feed shops. Talk to as many people you can about him. Keep an eye out for him on horses for sale pages and websites. If you see a grey in a field, check for the scar or other markings. It's the vigilance of people like you that will bring my boy home.

Take a look at Spirit's website. www.findspirit.co.uk. All his information is on there plus plenty of photos to identify him with. There is also the Facebook page which has around 9000 members. Just search for 'Spirit stolen!!! Please help find him!' It is a real shame that this book couldn't have a happy ending but consider it open ended as we never know if and when he may return. I hope I'll be writing a very happy sequel one day!

The following photos show Spirit's identifying marks that shouldn't change over time. One thing that will change about him though is his colouring. He was a lightly dappled grey when he was with me. Greys go whiter over the years so he is more than likely completely white now without the dapples. He may no longer have a long mane. The person he is with may have trimmed his mane short or hogged it completely and due to the fact that he is quite chunky he may look like a show cob.

I worry that I may not recognise him after all this time has passed but friends have reassured me that I will and that he would recognise me too. I think it's just a waiting game now to see if he appears up for sale or at a show or if a vet or farrier recognises him. All 47 passport issuing agencies in the UK are aware of him so I will be alerted if someone tries to get a passport for him under his current microchip number.

I understand that there is a possibility that he is no longer alive. If he isn't I just need to know. That way I can have closure and move on. But for as long as I believe he is alive I will keep searching.

If you have horses, please do everything you can to protect them from thieves. Horse theft is on the rise. They don't care what they take. They don't care how it affects the horses or their owners. Make sure your horses are microchipped and passported, freeze brand if you can. Take detailed photos of all identifying marks, any scars, whorls, striped feet etc. Take photos of both sides of your horse plus front and back and keep them in a safe place. All of these things will help should they take your horse. Put up CCTV where possible and keep gates locked at all times. I would never wish this experience on anyone as nearly five years on the theft of Spirit haunts me every day.

BUT LET'S STAY POSITIVE!!!.................LET'S FIND SPIRIT!!!!!!!!!

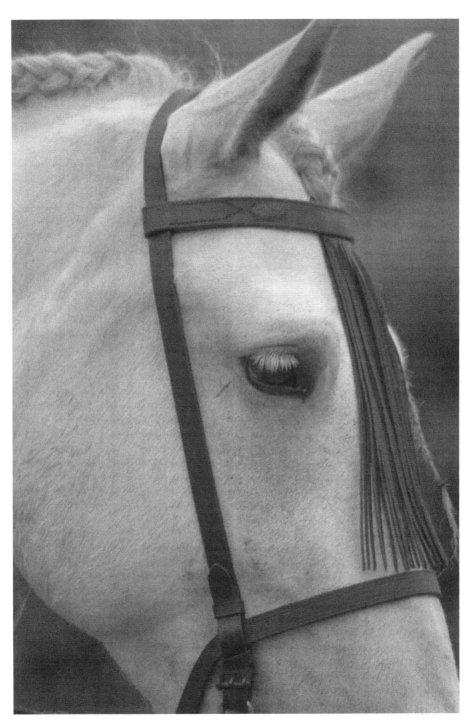

The scar below his right eye

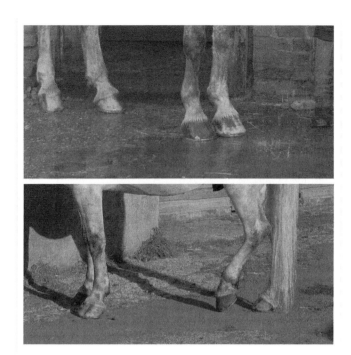

Distinctive feet

Small snip between nostrils

Find Spirit
£3000 REWARD!!!

Spirit is still missing after being stolen from his field in Carrington in 2011

With age he will have gone through some changes and could look quite different. The photos on the right show how he could have changed

He will most likely have lost his dapples and be a lot whiter. He may also be trimmed or hogged. The left shows his distinctive markings.

A small snip between his nostrils, distinctive feet, a large scar on the inside of his right hind leg and a small scar by his right eye.

Spirit is a 15.2hh Andalusian x gelding. He was born in 2003.

Please, please keep a look out and spread the word. Tell you farrier and you vet and other equine professionals.

This horse means the world to me and my life has been turned upside down since he was stolen. I miss him so so much!

There is a £3000 reward for information leading to the recovery of this horse. Please get in touch in confidence. Lisa Wasilewski 07712156726, lisa1121@googlemail.com or the police on 101 quoting reference 82762U/11.   www.findspirit.co.uk

www.findspirit.co.uk

Facebook - Spirit stolen!!! Please help find him!

The last photo I ever took of Spirit

Acknowledgements

I want to say a huge thank you to my mum who has supported me and my passion for horses all my life and for the massive amount of financial help she and my step dad have given me. She has always been there for me and has been a fantastic listener during the good and bad times. She has been my rock when I have felt like giving up. And an extra special thank you for her help and contributions to this book. Also thanks to my step dad and my brother who have been helping me along during tough times.

I also want to thank Helen Maybrey for being Spirit's second soul mate, for being there for me and for being a very special friend. I hate that we live so far away from each other now but our friendship is so strong it will never be an issue. Special thanks also for her help and contributions to this book.

Thank you also to Sarah Nash who has known Spirit for as long as I have. She has stood by my side for many years and I couldn't ask more from a friend.

Thank you to my lovely friend Joanne Roberts for giving me my first opportunity to get involved with Spanish horses. We have done so much together with our horses in the past and have many wonderful memories together.

Many thanks to Mark Rowston, my former partner who has been in the background through most of my story. Despite us no longer being together he is still a very good friend of mine and still supports me every day. Thank you for being in my life.

Just a few more individuals I want to thank. Sophie Nixon, Michelle Corrigan, Laura Wroe, Rebecca Brennand and Eileen, Sophie Griffin, Tracie Cini and Jill Murfin. They have all been involved with my horses at some stage. I appreciate all the support you have given me and all you have done to help me with my horses.

There are far too many other people for me to mention and thank here, in fact there are thousands, so an enormous thank you to each and every one of you who have contributed to the search for Spirit, who have stayed by my side through difficult times and who have given me hope and positivity for the future. Every share on Facebook, every message you have sent with a possible Spirit, every poster you have distributed, every farrier or vet you have told, thank you! It all contributes to bringing my special boy home.

I hope one day that Spirit will return, not just for me or for him, but for all of you. Thank you!

Lisa's mum here……..I was in a card shop a couple of years ago choosing a card for Lisa's birthday. At first glance one card looked just right because the front of it said "For my wonderful daughter" and the card had a fabulous picture on the front, but inside it described a daughter who was a success in all that she did. It said how proud this parent was of all her daughter's achievements through her life and that everything she turned her hand to she did well. I had to pull a tissue out of my handbag because tears immediately welled up in my eyes. - My precious daughter was trying so hard to cope with one loss after another at that time. How sad it was that everything my daughter tried to achieve was not turning out well for her. I bought a different card but then realised that I too could write in it how proud I was of my daughter……..for the great love she has for animals, especially horses, for the way she cares about them and makes sure their health issues aren't neglected and that their wellbeing is a priority. I'm also proud of her for keeping going when she's wanted to give up on life. So on that birthday I told her how proud I was of all that she's overcome. She may not be a doctor or a solicitor, etc., but she has achieved so very much in her life and will continue to do so. If anyone reading this thinks they haven't achieved a great deal in their life, please think again, and celebrate all your accomplishments (big and small) and for hanging-in there when life is tough. Not all achievements come in the form of things the world considers success.

Printed in Great Britain
by Amazon